Green Power 2010: David's Stone

Green Power 2010:
Davids Stone

Erik A Broenau

United States
2010

ISBN: 1-451-588-771/EAN-13: 9-781-451-588-774

Dedication
My parents, family, friends and Apollo.

Table of Contents

Introduction

The information presented is based on real events that happen to average people in America every day. David was violated, burglarized and vandalized by someone still unidentified then violated again by multi-billion dollar corporate America because of this unidentified culprits activity. Refusing to just sit back in silence he started researching, learning, identifying, and creating a strategy to overcome the violation. Florida residents as an example, one of the highest unemployment rates in the nation having a significant crime rate compared with the rest of the nation and one of the highest populations collecting Social Security are being legally violated by corporate America. There are people in worse financial situations; this struggle represents those in the proverbial donut hole, living pay check to pay check, praying, hoping and wishing that nothing unforeseen happens while being legally violated. He followed the money trail and it is unbelievable what he found all of it legal.

Information and knowledge is power. Alone this will do nothing but a collective effort would send a message that we the people do have a say and control in what is under our own domain. If you get bored with narratives, definitions, facts, and a simple solution then this is not for you. Are you willing to take control of what is under your own domain? *Are you interested in reducing your electric cost by 56.5% a month?*

Historical Data	Last Month	1 Yr Ago	KWH This Month	KWH Per Day
2/04-3/02/10	7393	1679	875	34
3/02-4/01/10	875	253	143	5
4/02-5/03/10	143	----	----	----

David or Goliath

    December, January, and February for 2009 and 2010 the electrical power bill rumors began to surface. The public soon learned it was not rumors. It was not uncommon to see a power bill of $250.00 or greater. Hundreds of families sought help with their bill increasing the demand on public assistance. Fact, one power bill was $800.85 (7393 KWH) for the month of January 2010. The individual sought public assistance and was told, *we cannot help you this is too much.* You can imagine what David was thinking when he saw an electric bill for $800.85.

    Simplifying, we will name this individual David and the electrical company Goliath. The highest usage David had received in the past was March 2008 (1090 KWH), January 2009 (1831 KWH), February 2009 (1679 KWH), June 2009 (1481 KWH), January 2010 (2018 KWH) and January 2010 (7393 KWH). Yes, in a three day period in January 2010 the electrical usage basically quadrupled. How could that be?

    David was aware that the electric bill would be in the upper range for December 2009 because it was cold and received a December bill for $9.99 paying approximately $60.00 aware something was not right and believed it was a partial monthly billing. January 2010, David received an electrical bill for $214.00; this was more in line with what David thought it should be and believed it was the December bill. February 2, 2010, David received a correspondence from the electric company stating the electric meter required to be read at least once every six months according to the public service commission. The meter could not be read because it was: *Inaccessible-Fence Locked.* David had a problem, first the meter was not behind a locked fence and in the twenty years of residing at the same address the meter has never been behind a fence. David called the number conveyed in the correspondence to arrange for a meter reading immediately as requested. The electric company explained that it might have been a group of trainees learning the job or a sub-contractor who was unfamiliar with the location of the meter. The electric company also stated that occasionally they use and employ trainees and sub-contractors, because it is more cost effective to the companys bottom line. David understood reducing costs in todays economy. Three days after receiving the January 2010 bill for $214.00 he received a bill for $800.85. Later when the electric company performed the free energy audit they changed the reason for not being able to read the meter because of a privacy bush. The meter could have been read had the meter reader walked an additional twenty or twenty-five feet to access the meter without the privacy bush present. Coincidentally this same privacy bush has been in the same place for the last two years and meter readings occurred.

David then sought public assistance with this bill. David supplied his W2 statements for 2009. The public assistance personnel stated the W2 was not an acceptable proof of income and could not be accepted only the Social Security Awards letter and the Insurance letter would be acceptable. David provided the Social Security Awards letter issued each year and the Insurance Awards letter. Public assistance gross annual allowable income for public assistance is: $16, 245.00. David pays Medicare Premiums each month and his income was $344.16 a year more than is allowed by public assistance. You cannot receive public assistance if you have the disconnection notice in hand.

David goes to New York during the summer months to help his aging parents and be out of harms way during Hurricane Season. David always turns the power off at the breaker box before leaving. However, upon Davids return in December 2009 there was a surprise waiting. Davids residence of 20 plus years had been burglarized and vandalized. David called the Sheriff's department immediately. The CSU (Crime Scene Unit) was dispatched and procedures implemented for the incident. David contacted the insurance company to learn that he was not covered for burglary and vandalism and even if he was it would not be covered because he had not been in the residence for more than 30 days. David estimates approximately $5,500.00 worth of items had been stolen such as heavy duty extension cords, tools, computers, televisions, cameras, lawn mower, and personal information. David amended the crime report to include the electric bill. The bill was returned and the officer explained it could not be used in the report of items stolen. Why not? David was told to not expect this crime to be resolved quickly because it is not a television show and the limited number of serial numbers David had for the items stolen. Oddly the year before Davids $3000.00 generator was stolen with a serial number and still not recovered. This did not include the total disarray of the household. Davids neighbors did not see anything or notice anything but there was a rash of burglaries in the vicinity.

Electrical service is a necessity today versus receiving a disconnect notice he took action ahead of time to prevent this from happening. David called the public service commission regarding the electric bill and they put David in contact with a representative of the electric company. David explained to the public service commission and the electric company representative the circumstances and situation. David knowing electric service is a necessity worked with the electric company to arrive at a workable payment schedule to prevent a disconnection based on the limited and fixed income he has. The electric company sent a supervisor out to demonstrate how to read the electric meter so David could monitor the usage and scheduled a free energy audit. He wrote letters to everyone he could think of including the electric utility company and their response was there is nothing they can do but authorize a repayment plan. David was not contesting the estimated usage for December of 1564 KWH ($201.89) or the estimated usage for January of 1374 KWH ($178.27). David was contesting the 1469 KWH estimated usage for September, 1469 KWH estimated usage for October, and 1422 KWH estimated usage for November in a total amount of $542.12 while David was in New York.

David, having made payment arrangements to avoid being disconnected then had to make drastic changes to compensate for the electric bill and losses. The electric company insisted that David should be comfortable in his home. How can David be comfortable with an $800.00 electric bill still due? Once David saw this electric bill, which was approximately the 10th or 11th of February 2010 he elected to take extreme action. How many cold advisories were posted after this date? The next electric bill David received was 875 KWH, $166.62, which included the repayment agreement plus taxes. Had David not taken these extreme measures he would have faced another $200.00 plus the agreement for the electric bill. David by now has reached a point of frustration, anger, being overwhelmed, and feeling helpless. David will soon be facing the reverse conditions, high humidity and high temperatures, more difficult to compensate and adjust for versus cold temperatures unless you are a cold blooded creature.

David contacted his State Representative and initially they listened to the story regarding the events and public assistance. David called back twice with an update, the number was taken but calls were never returned. David contacted his Congressmans office and they suggested contacting State Representative office and the State Public Service Commission. David was already two steps ahead.

Unions, Pensions and Security

The 21st century will be defined by the technology revolution, the Internet and computerization just as the 18th and 19th centuries were defined by the Industrial Revolution. The Industrial Revolution was not without side effects, Upton Sinclair (Wikipedia, 2010) wrote The Jungle in 1906 describing the working conditions of the Chicago meat packing industry. This led to the passage of the Meat Inspection Act, the Pure Food and Drug Act, the eventual creation of the Food and Drug Administration (FDA) in 1930, and the socialist concept of Unions and the unionization movement by employees to guarantee safe working conditions, a modest income, and other work related issues. The U.S. Congress established a Bureau of Labor in 1888; President Taft in 1913 upgraded this to the Department of Labor, a Cabinet level department (Wikipedia, 2010). The task of the U.S. Department of Labor has the same purpose as a Union. President Roosevelt introduced the Social Security Act in 1935 as part of the New Deal; it was merged into the Cabinet level Federal Security Agency. Then, in 1953 it was placed under the Department of Health, Education and Welfare. President Clinton signed a law in 1994 changing the status of the Social Security Administration and placing it within the executive branch of government (Wikipedia, 2010).

Wikipedia (Wikipedia, 2010) describes pensions as financial vehicles that provide and income to people when they are no longer earning a regular income. There are employment based pensions, social and state pensions, and disability pensions. Social Security, IRAs and 401(k) plans are all examples of pensions varying in the methods they are funded in some instances funded by a Labor Union, some funded by the individual themselves, some a combined contribution of the employee and employer, and some by payroll taxes. Federal and State government employees are eligible to receive benefits under the Federal Retirement System or the Civil Service Retirement System. The most recognizable unions in the United States are the AFL-CIO and UAW. The most underfunded pension system in the United States is Social Security while the best pensions are for government employees and union employees.

Federal, State, and County government employees are employed by the public via the routing, re-routing and channeling of tax revenues. In short, their entire earnings are funded by federal, state, local taxes and fees such as income tax, property tax, sales tax, and regulated licenses. They themselves pay into the Social Security System, as everyone does, the FICA payroll deduction. They may or may not contribute to their pensions. Yet, their pensions are guaranteed. The State of New York facing a significant budget crisis, as many States are, must fund these pensions by law. Then, they retire and move to a State which does not have an income tax and live comfortably until they pass away. Why are their spouses or partners eligible to collect their pension benefits? Why are their children eligible to collect their pension benefits? Why are they able to collect Social Security too?

The Department of Labor and Unions have similar tasks regarding the welfare and treatment of the American employee. The Department of Labor funded by taxes and the Unions funded at least by dues paid mandated for membership. Unions are protected by law and in some instances the State must contract a job to a unionized company even when they could possibly contract the job to a non-unionized company at a lesser cost to the tax payer. Corporate giants such as Ford, GM, and Chrysler, are major employers in the United States with an enormous union representation in the United Auto Workers Union (UAW). Corporations have to make a profit to employ their employees and cover overhead, such as paying their utility bill. The Union engages in contract negotiations securing job benefits, hourly wages, job descriptions, and union dues for its members. The corporations then have to offset and create a means to meet these financial obligations resulting in the increased cost of the items to consumers. Basically, this action impacts the national inflation rate and cost of living allowance (COLA) which is then examined by the government.

Individual Retirement Accounts (IRAs) and 401(k) plans are funded by individuals and their employer. IRAs receive their primary contribution from individuals depositing a percentage of their monthly income and is completely voluntary. The funds accumulated can be invested in various stocks listed on the Stock Exchanges of their choice or can remain in cash deposits. Conversely, 401(k) plans are funded by the individual and their employer but investments on the Stock Exchange are predetermined and *only approved investment* venues are available. Enron Corporation was one of those approved energy investment venues (Wikipedia, 2001).

These are a few of the financial vehicles available to the American people to prepare for the future. There appears to be duplicity of purpose and function within Government and Corporate America, or this could be viewed as choice, or a system of checks and balances. There are a multiple venues to provide at the least a minimum income for every American, be it funded by payroll taxes, corporations and unions, or the individual themselves. Retirement vehicles totally funded by the individual, such as IRAs, or the individuals contributing portion of 401(k)s, should never be denied to the spouse, partner, family member (child or sibling), relative (within reason such as a first cousin), or mandated to be publically distributed. However, the corporate contributions to 401(k)s should be distributed into the Social Security System upon the specific employees death. *Social Security is the most underfunded retirement vehicle available to Americans and demand is increasing.* That is not what it initially was set up to become but in reality that is what it has become.

Definitions: Fine line or Power line

Webster (Merriam-Webster, 2010) defines a monopoly as the: 1: exclusive ownership through legal privilege, command of supply, or concerted action, 2: exclusive possession or control, 3: a commodity controlled by one party, 4: one that has a monopoly. **Extortion is:** 1: the act or practice of extorting especially money or other property; especially: the offense committed by an official engaging in such practice, 2: something extorted; especially: a gross overcharge **(Merriam-Webster, 2010). Bribe is defined as,** 1: money or favor given or promised in order to influence the judgment or conduct of a person in a position of trust, 2: something that serves to influence or induce **(Merriam-Webster, 2010). Lobbyist are,** : to conduct activities aimed at influencing public officials and especially members of a legislative body on legislation, 1: to promote (as a project) or secure the passage of (as legislation) by influencing public officials, 2: to attempt to influence or sway (as a public official) toward a desired action **(Merriam-Webster, 2010). Capitalism is,** : an economic system characterized by private or corporate ownership of capital goods, by investments that are determined by private decisions, and by prices, production, and the distribution of goods that are determined mainly by competition in a free market **(Merriam-Webster, 2010). Free markets are,** an economic market operating by free competition **(Merriam-Webster, 2010). Competition is,** 1: the act or process of competing: rivalry as a: the effort of two or more parties acting independently to secure the business of a third party by offering the most favorable terms, b: active demand by two or more organisms or kinds of organisms for some environmental resource in short supply, 2: a contest between rivals **(Merriam-Webster, 2010). Crimes against humanity is an:** : atrocity (as extermination or enslavement) that is directed especially against an entire population or part of a population on specious grounds and without regard to individual guilt or responsibility even on such grounds (Merriam-Webster, 2010).

A monopoly within the context of economics is described as a situation where an individual or enterprise has sufficient control over a product or service and determine the rules that others may have access to it (Wikipedia, 2010). Characteristics of a monopoly include a single seller and market power. They can emerge as a result of economic barriers, control of natural resources, legal barriers and deliberate action. In determining whether an entity is acting as a monopoly or in the spirit of a competitive market factors such as market power, product differentiation, number of competitors, barriers to entry, PED, excess profits, profit maximization, P-Max quantity, price and profit are guides. The government is empowered to create and authorize legal monopolies, copyrights, patents, and trademarks are common examples.

Economic monopolies are complex with the rules, characteristics, technicalities and guidelines established under competition law. Wikipedia (Wikipedia, 2010) suggests that while an entity exhibits a large market share it does not mean a customer, client, or consumer is paying in excess for the particular commodity. The law creates categories for behaviors which are generally prohibited such as limiting supply, predatory pricing, price discrimination, refusal to deal and exclusive dealing, dividing territories, tying commerce and product bundling. Dividing territories is described as an agreement by two companies to stay out of each other's way and reduce competition in the agreed-upon territories (Wikipedia, 2010). It is one of several anti-competitive practices in the United States. The term is generally understood to include dividing customers as well (Wikipedia, 2010). These are identified as anti-competitive practices. It seems logical and prudent that this type of agreement would likely be a verbal agreement happening during board meetings rather than leaving an evidentiary paper trail.

Corporate Goliath

Green power seems to be a euphemism applicable to Wall Street. The public mantra is green, green, and greener. The reality is a few enjoy green power while many continue to lose their homes and face potential unemployment. Publicly traded energy titans The American Electric Power, Inc. (AEP), Dominion Resources, Inc. (D), Duke Energy Corporation (DUK), Entergy Corporation (ETR), FPL Group (FPL), First Energy Corporation (FE), Edison International (EIX) and The Southern Company (SO) are reaping profits with no end in sight. We can presume non-public traded companies in the same market caps are performing equally well. Electric utilities are a necessity in the 21st century equivalent to basic needs described by Maslows Hierarchy such as food and shelter. Why are we being taxed on our utilities?

These companies are profiting on the backs of America, paying quarterly dividends to their shareholders and beating Wall Street estimates with regularity. Wall Street predictions or estimates are determined by several financial analysts who take into consideration a number of factors that may influence the earnings a particular company might have every three months. The Southern Company beat Wall Street estimates in five consecutive quarters, Dominion Resources beat estimates six consecutive quarters, Duke Energy beat estimates five of four consecutive quarters, FPL Group five consecutive quarters, American Electric Power five consecutive quarters, Entergy Corporation five consecutive quarters, First Energy five consecutive quarters, and Edison International with five consecutive quarters according to E*Trade (E*Trade, 2010).

Yahoo Finance (Yahoo Finance, 2010) identifies *three common major shareholders The Black Rock Institutional Trust Company, N.A., a second as The Vanguard Group Inc., and third as State Street Corporation* (STT) *in each of these electric utilities*.

It should be noted that in determining the composite views for Figure 1 and Figure 2 only Major Institutional Share Holders shown values on Yahoo were used in the calculation. The values were obtained by adding the total shares held by institutional investors State Street Corporation, Blackrock Institutional Trust Company, N.A., and The Vanguard Group plus the total number of Other Institutional shares held. Then, total shares held by State Street Corporation, Black Rock Institutional Trust Company, N.A. and The Vanguard Group were divided by the overall total number of shares resulting in the percentages. (See Figure 1 and Figure 2)

Each receive a minimum of .31 per share through a maximum of .75 per share for a low estimate of *$68,229,360.41* on a total of 220,094,711 shares every three months, State Street alone, received this potential payment on dividends. Other major *institutional share holders of State Street Corporation include* (Yahoo Finance, 2010), *The Black Rock Institutional Trust Company, N.A., The Vanguard Group Inc.*, Massachusetts Financial Services Co-Other, Capital Research Global Investors, FMR LLC., Price (T.Rowe) Associates Inc., Putnam Investment Management LLC, General Electric Company and *State Street Corporation* itself. State Street Corporation has beat Wall Street estimates for eleven consecutive quarters (almost three years) paying a quarterly dividend of .01 per share to shareholders.

State Street Corporation is also a major holder of shares in oil companies like Conoco Phillips (COP), Exxon Mobil Corp (XOM), Chevron Corporation (CVX), and BP plc (BP) also paying quarterly dividends. E*Trade (E*Trade, 2010) reports COP beat Wall Street estimates for 9 consecutive quarters and paying .50 per share this quarter for 55,720,470 shares, XOM beat Wall Street estimates 4 of 9 consecutive quarters and paying .42 per share this quarter for 179,651,376 shares, CVX beat Wall Street estimates 4 of 9 consecutive quarters paying .68 per share this quarter for 96,958,660 shares, and BP beat Wall Street estimates 6 of 9 consecutive quarters paying .84 per share this quarter for 42,729,671 shares, where total shares is 375,060,177 and *received a minimum overall dividend of $157,525,274.34 million based on a minimum of .42 per share on oil conglomerates and $68,229,360.41 million based on a minimum of .31 per share on utility giants every three months*. The Black Rock Institutional Trust Company, N.A. and The Vanguard Group Inc would receive a similar quarterly dividend (excluding any dividend payment by BP plc). *The Black Rock Institutional Trust Company, N.A. is a significant shareholder of State Street Corporation.*

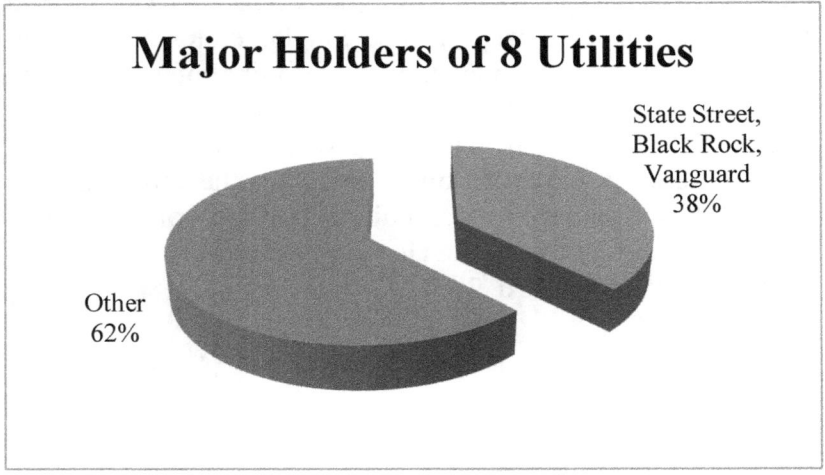

Figure 1: Composite View of Utility Shareholders

The rule on Wall Street is buy shares low and sell shares high, there are rules established regarding the quantity any investor is allowed to trade during any interim of time. However, if and when these Institutional Investors buy 10,000 shares of Acme Thumbtack Co for $2.50 when the Stock Exchange opens, sell it for $3.50 before the Stock Exchange closes that same day, they have made $10,000.00 in profit in 8 hours or less. *That is not even close to 1% of the total shares they hold and the profit on the sale is at least 50% of what many Social Security recipients have as a Gross Income.*

Technically, The Black Rock Institutional Trust Company, N.A., The Vanguard Group and State Street Corporation are not a monopoly in and of themselves just because they are common major holders of numerous shares in Electric, Oil, and Oil Refining conglomerates. Institutional and Mutual Funds own 43% of Southern Company, 58% of Dominion Resources, Inc., 51% of Duke Energy Corporation, 65% of FPL Group, Inc., 71% of American Electric Power, Inc., 79% of Entergy Corporation, 73% of First Energy Corporation, 76% of Edison International, 73% of Conoco Phillips, 49% of Exxon Mobil Corporation, 63% of Chevron Corporation, and 11% of BP plc Common Stock, and 75% of Valero Energy Corporation (VLO) (Yahoo , 2010). (See Figure 2) Obviously, in a majority of these conglomerates Institutional and mutual fund owners maintain a controlling interest able to influence any and all aspects of corporate initiatives and policy legally. The general public and small share holder rarely hold enough shares to influence policy, much less the ability to unite to approve or disapprove a particular action most of the time such as the case involving the Hewlett Packard-Compaq merger (Hewlett Packard, 2001).

Zacks (Zacks Equity Research, 2010) reported State Street Corporation paid its leaving CEO 5.4 million in cash and AP (Associated Press, 2010) reported they had spent a total of $480,000.00 to lobby financial and regulation reform in Washington, D.C., during the 3rd and 4th quarters of 2009. Holding a significant number of shares in eight electric utility companies, four major oil companies, and an oil refinery creates an enormous market share with tremendous voting power regarding policies within each of these companies and a significant national influence in Congress. It also empowers these large corporations with the ability to employ efficient

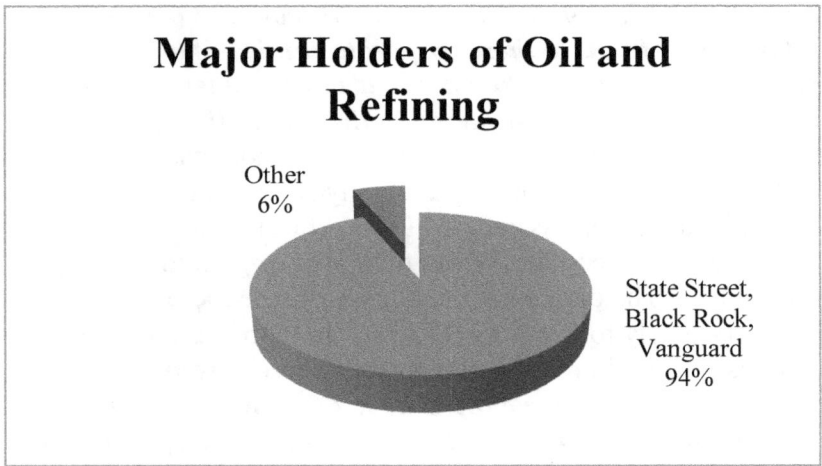

Figure 2: Composite View of Oil and Refining Shareholders

accountants and lawyers to explain and account for millions in dividend income and billions in revenue during a recession crushing the average American.

Monopolies, extortion, and bribery are illegal in the United States. They are probably even more difficult to prove and demonstrate in a court of law. *We have to ask at what point do the actions of corporate America become criminal or crimes against humanity when the average person is losing their home as a result of foreclosure and unemployment, the CEO's walk away with more money than the majority will earn in a lifetime, and banks will not lend to the people regardless of reason based on a credit score but they will allow TARP funds to these corporate entities. While the government continues to not include or consider the cost of energy as an aspect considered in the cost of living.* The Supreme Court of the United States even understands obscenity (Silver, 2010), while the dog and pony show is broadcast by the national media (Associated Press, 2005). Businesses continue to lay people off from their jobs or go into bankruptcy themselves. The demand on public assistance increases proportionately to home foreclosures and job loss and energy moguls wallow in more green power. *There is something wrong when corporate entities have the power to create and manipulate the environment where it is not cost effective to heat or cool your home and drive to work to support yourself or your family.* When does this become criminal? When can charges be filed? When can it be prosecuted? When does it stop? Where does it stop?

Corporations and Unemployment

It is difficult to understand how the national unemployment rate can be as high as it is. The companies providing a necessity such as electricity for appliances from refrigerators to computers routinely report revenue in the billions. *It is socially irresponsible (ethically and morally) for corporations to continue this profiteering while the average American continues to face job loss, home foreclosure and property depreciation.*

American Electric Power Inc. (AEP), Dominion Resources, Inc. (D), Duke Energy Corporation (DUK), Edison International (EIX) Entergy Corporation (ETR), FPL Group (FPL), First Energy Corporation (FE), and The Southern Company (SO), provide electrical services to an enormous population. American Electric Power (American Electric Power, 2010) provides electrical resources to AEP Ohio, AEP Texas, Indiana Michigan Power, Kentucky Power, and Appalachian Power covering Tennessee, Virginia, and West Virginia. Dominion Resources (Dominion Companies, 2010) electrical distribution are identified as Dominion North Carolina Power and Dominion Virginia Power. Duke Energy Corporation (Duke Energy Corporation, 2010) includes Duke Energy of Indiana, Duke Energy Carolinas, Duke Energy Ohio and Duke Energy Kentucky. Edison International (Edison International, 2010) serves California. Entergy Corporation (Entergy Corporation, 2010) includes 10 subsidiaries. First Energy Corporation (First Energy Corporate, 2010) includes Jersey Central Power and Light, Metropolitan Edison Company, Ohio Edison Company, Pennsylvania Electric Company, Pennsylvania Power Company, The Cleveland Electric Illuminating Company, and the Toledo Edison Company. FPL Group is present in Florida, Canada, and 27 other states (FPL Group, 2010). Finally, the Southern Company (The Southern Company, 2010) is comprised of seven subsidiaries. (See Appendix Utilities for their subsidiaries and corresponding unemployment rates in the states they operate) (Bureau of Labor Statistics, 2010).

Eight electric utility corporations being traded on Wall Street we have to ask questions about past, present and future earnings in *revenue. There are billions of dollars in revenue* E*Trade (E*Trade, 2010) .

Company Symbol	Actual Revenue 2009	Projected Revenue 2010	Projected Revenue 2011	Billion/Year
AEP	13.5B	14.9B	15.5B	
D	15.1B	16.0B	16.5B	
DUK	12.7B	13.6B	14.4B	
FPL	15.6B	16.7B	17.2B	
FE	13.0B	14.1B	14.6B	
EIX	12.4B	13.6B	14.0B	
ETR	6.67B	6.72B	7.12B	
SO	15.7B	17.0B	17.8B	
Total(s)	104.67			Billion 2009
		112.62		Billion 2010
			117.12	Billion 2011

FPL Group had 15.6 Billion in revenue for 2009, and an estimated 16.7 Billion for 2010 and 17.2 Billion for 2011. Southern Company had 15.7 Billion for 2009, estimated 17 Billion for 2010, and an estimated 17.8 Billion for 2011 in revenue. That is 104.6 Billion in combined actual revenue in 2009; 112.62 Billion estimated revenue for 2010; and a total projected 117.12 Billion dollars in revenue for 2011 in eight utility companies covering 18 of the 50 States.

State Street Corporation (STT) is a significant institutional investor in these publicly traded companies operating in 18 of the 50 United States, *10 of the 18 States have the highest rates of unemployment in the nation* (See Appendix Utilities), and announced it has repaid its *2 Billion dollars in TARP funding* (State Street Corporate, 2009). Holding significant shares in so many utility companies enables them to vote and influence corporate operations and policies, and accountants ensure they pay the minimum for their Federal and State estimated taxes. *Their annual revenue for 2009 was 8.8 Billion, an estimated 9.1 Billion for 2010, and 9.9 Billion for 2011* (E*Trade, 2010). What was their intent *lobbying in Washington* on financial reform the 3rd and 4th quarter of 2009 immediately following the repayment of *received TARP funding*? They beat Wall Street estimates for the past 11 quarters (almost 3 years). The public will never know. Figure 3 displays the closing prices on Wall Street for all the publically traded companies presented in this document for April 1, 2010.

Company Name	Symbol	Price	Chg
AMERICAN ELEC PWR INC COM	AEP	34.49	0.31
BP P L C SPONSORED ADR	BP	57.74	0.67
CONOCOPHILLIPS COM	COP	52.02	0.85
CHEVRON CORP NEW COM	CVX	76.69	0.86
DOMINION RES INV VA NEW COM	D	41.83	0.72
DUKE ENERGY CORP NEW COM	DUK	16.41	0.09
EDISON INTL COM	EIX	34.30	0.13
ENTERGY CORP NEW COM	ETR	82.32	0.97
FIRSTENERGY CORP COM	FE	39.46	0.37
FPL GROUP INC COM	FPL	48.84	0.51
SOUTHERN CO COM	SO	33.42	0.26
STATE STR CORP COM	STT	45.97	0.83
VALERO ENERGY CORP NEW COM	VLO	20.02	0.32
EXXON MOBIL CORP COM	XOM	67.61	0.63

Figure 3: April 1 2010 Closing Price

Government Protection

A Public Service Commission is available for each state within the United States designated to ensure that consumers receive essential basic services such as electric, gas, phone and water. They have the authority to oversee and regulate utility companies in basic areas such as: rate base/economic regulation, competitive market oversight, and monitoring of safety, reliability, and services (My Florida Public Service Commission, 2010). These are public records available to everyone where you can learn what is and what are not acceptable actions of the part of a utility company (My Florida Public Service Commission, 2010). Generally, the Public Service Commission will provide a means to contact them (My Florida Public Service Commission, 2010) and when or what concerns to contact them about (My Florida Public Service Commission, 2010). For example, if you tamper with your electric meter to somehow alter its operation it is a Theft of Services on the Utility Company. However, if someone burglarizes, vandalizes, and runs your kWh usage through the roof it is Theft of Services you have to pay for out of your pocket. The utility companies are required to submit an annual financial report of operations every year. For example, Gulf Power, a subsidiary of the Southern Company is required to submit their quarterly financial reports (Gulf Power, 2009). I have to ask why the Public Service Commissions are not mandating a reduction in the cost of utilities or denying rate increases for the utility companies in areas of high unemployment versus requesting and approving an increase (Angier, 2008) (Market Watch-The Wall Street Journal, 2010) while these corporations continue to reap billions of revenues annually and pay quarterly dividends to shareholders.

The Florida Public Service Commission (FPSC) has authority to regulate numerous public services such as railroads, telephone, motor carriers, telegraph, gas, electric, water and sewage companies organizational operations, procedure and regulate themselves (Florida Department of State, 2010). Their application and scope is designed to promote good business practices and establish the rights and responsibilities for both the electric utility and the consumer (Florida Department of State, 2010). This appears to cover every facet from the consumer to the generation of power.

FPSC has established meter readings by the utility company since at least 1980 and are to occur monthly unless there are special circumstances and at least once every six months (Florida Department of State, 2010). Utility companies are required to maintain accurate records regarding the history of each meter. A customer can request one meter testing within a 12 months period without incurring a fee or possible service charge resulting from the test. A refereed meter reading can be requested in the event of a dispute between the utility company and the customer. This usually qualifies as a complaint and the utility companies must keep on file or record every written complaint they receive. The procedure implemented to determine if there is a problem with the meter is based on an algebraic average formula and the utility company selects the method which is the best fit to the customers usage pattern. In the case of unauthorized or fraudulent use, the utility company, based on a reasonable estimate, can bill the customer. When, there is sufficient cause, estimated billing can be implemented for up to three consecutive months and then the utility company is required to contact the customer to explain why it is being estimated. Right of way and easements must be suitable to the utility. Territorial agreements require the utility companies to submit a qualified map of the proposed area, identifying the class of people to be affected, they be notified of any potential rate differences, and the results from a voting procedure. Conversely, territorial disputes require a qualified map, the utilities capabilities, nature of the disputed area as in urban or rural, and costs to the utility for distribution. If, these factors are equal then customer preference plays a role in resolving the dispute. These are just a few of the rules established by FPSC (Florida Department of State, 2010).

The State of Florida provides support for the Victims of Crime (VOC) (Florida Attorney General, 2010) starting with a Victims Services Directory for each of the counties (Florida Attorney General, 2010). The Victims Compensation Brochure (Florida Attorney General, 2010) explains the benefits available, who is eligible to apply for a victim, information required to apply, and who qualifies as victim and the qualification requirements. Instructions on how to file for victims compensation are provided on their site if you pass the qualification process (Florida Attorney General, 2010). Compensation and recovery assistance is available for a wide variety of crimes from A to Z.

Available benefits include wage loss, disability, funeral expenses, treatment expenses, and domestic violence relocation. The victim, intervener, guardian, sibling or spouse of a victim can make the request for application. One of the pre-requisites to qualify for compensation as a victim of theft or burglary is your home owners insurance policy does not cover the loss. If, someone violates you, vandalizing and stealing personal property from your home you are eligible to seek compensation if you are 60 or older or disabled. If, the perpetrator uses your electricity (unauthorized and fraudulent use of a utility) this is not an item that qualifies as something you are able to receive compensation or recovery assistance as a victim of a crime (See Appendix Resources PSC and VOC for information specific to your State).

Currently, individuals, families, multi-housing units and businesses pay the same rate for their kWh usage each month; it could be .10 per kWh, .12 per kWh, or .14 per kWh dependent on what the PSC for your area has determined. What is the proportion of your monthly income under this rate system being spent on electric utilities? Imagine the percentage of your monthly income in fuel costs for your vehicle.

Fixed kWh Rate X Variable Income for Electric Utilities

Monthly Income (after deductions) Based on W2 Statement	Monthly kWh Usage	Fixed Rate per kWh not based on Monthly Income	Variable % of Monthly Income
Monthly kWh Usage x Fixed Rate per kWh			
$1000.00	500	.12	6.0%
$1500.00	500	.12	4.0%
$2000.00	500	.12	3.0%
$2500.00	500	.12	2.4%
$3000.00	500	.12	2.0%
$3500.00	500	.12	1.72%
$4000.00	500	.12	1.5%
$4500.00	500	.12	1.33%
$5000.00	500	.12	1.2%
$10000.00	500	.12	.6%

Source: Fictitious data, for illustration purposes only

Monthly Income (after deductions) Based on W2 Statement	Monthly kWh Usage	Variable Rate per kWh based on Monthly Income	Fixed % of Monthly Income
Monthly kWh Usage x Variable Rate per kWh			
$1000.00	500	.06	3.0%
$1500.00	500	.09	3.0%
$2000.00	500	.12	3.0%
$2500.00	500	.15	3.0%
$3000.00	500	.18	3.0%
$3500.00	500	.21	3.0%
$4000.00	500	.24	3.0%
$4500.00	500	.27	3.0%
$5000.00	500	.30	3.0%
$10000.00	500	.60	3.0%

Source: Fictitious data, for illustration purposes only

Electric utilities are a necessity not a luxury. ***Why since the introduction of Solar Energy are these utilities not mandated*** *by the State or engaging in a concerted effort to decentralize power production, the control of power distribution, reduce demand on fossil fuels, reduce the production of waste from nuclear power production and provide customer financing to have grid-tied solar roofing or panels installed in homes?* Billions of dollars in actual and estimated revenue is a strong possibility (Clean Energy.Org, 2009). Coincidentally in reviewing the PSC web site and speaking with a PSC representative: 1) I was unable to locate anywhere stating that a Utility Company was not allowed to credit, dismiss, refund, or place into their balance sheet losses, an Act of Theft of Services when the consumer is the victim. 2) The PSC representative stated a credit, dismissal or refund was up to the total discretion of the utility company. *Where are the protections for the consumer and victims of crime against legal monopolies, unauthorized use, fraudulent use, excessive billing and lazy meter readers?*

Basic Electric Breaker Box

Every home and business has a breaker box located somewhere within it. Figure 4, is a depiction of a common breaker box. It has a long horizontal breaker commonly referred to as the Main Breaker and is the main on-off switch for their respective location. The circuit breakers below vary in the amount of amperage they allow to pass through and control different electrical services and appliances within your home. The left cover panel initially has blank lines where you can write the circuit breaker place number and the corresponding room(s), location(s), or appliances it controls you should document this information for troubleshooting and future reference. The place numbers are usually embossed or engraved to the left or the right of the circuit breaker slot. These circuit breakers are safety mechanisms to prevent overload and a potential fire. They can also act as a trouble shooting mechanism. For example, the breaker in slot 1 might service the master bathroom of your home. If, you turn on your hair dryer it causes the breaker to trip and power is immediately turned off to your bathroom. This could indicate another problem in your house wiring or indicate you have exceeded the maximum capacity for the circuit breaker. The safest way to determine the cause is to consult a licensed electrician.

Figure 4: Breaker Box

How to Read Your Electric Meter

Your electric meter is used by your utility company to determine the number of kWh you have used to determine and calculate your bill. This number is derived by subtracting the last previous good reading from the current reading. There are a variety of electric meter types such as numeric display meters, electromechanical or standard meter, variable rate meter, prepayment electric meter, solid state electric meter, and electronic meters (Article Cube, 2010). Your Public Service Commission determines the minimum number of times a meter must be read for a particular time interim. It may have to be read by regulations every month, every three months or every six months. The most common electric meter is an electromechanical or standard meter and what will be presented here.

Figure 5: Electromechanical or Standard Electric Meter

An electromechanical or standard meter displays five circles with numerical entries one through zero and a pointing indicator in each one. The pointing indicators rotate in alternating and opposite direction and at a different rate of speed reflective of the amount or quantity of kilowatt hours (kWh) used in your home. Conceptually this is akin to measuring time in increments of days, hours, minutes, seconds, and milliseconds. The electric meter presented in Figure 5 identifies (A), (B), (C), (D), and (E) each with an arrow preceding them. A rotates clockwise, B rotates counter-clock wise, and C rotates clock wise, D rotates counter clock wise, E rotates clock wise, the slowest rotation occurs in A and the fastest rotation occurs in E, this is reflective of the magnitude or amount of measuring or tracking your usage of kWh.

Seco Energy (Seco Energy, 2010) directions state, When standing directly in front of your electric meter you will see five dials, that each look similar to a clock. Too get the correct reading begin at the far right and read to the left and write the numbers down as you go. When a hand is between two numbers, record the lower number. If you can⊟ decide if the hand is directly on the number, as reflected on dial E below, look at the dial to the right. If the hand on the dial to the right has passed 0 write down the number the hand is on for the dial in question. If the hand on the dial to the right has not passed 0, write down the lower number for the dial in question. For example, since the hand in dial D has not passed 0, dial E is 2.

Following these directions and applying it to Figure 5 you might write 44641. A couple weeks pass and you⊟re going out to check your meter and usage and you repeat the process writing down 54641, wait another two weeks and record 64641. Fantastic, you have just recorded the values to calculate the kWh used in your home and can estimate your electric bill. You grab your calculator or pencil and paper, subtracting 44641 from 64641 and arrive at 20,000 kWh of usage for the month. About now you are saying to yourself something is wrong, there is absolutely no way I could use this much electricity in a month and have absolutely no idea how you are going to be able to pay the amount you have calculated. It is no wonder these utility companies have billions in revenue each year.

The directions provided are correct and will result in the correct meter readings with the understanding of what happened. Most people in America read and write from left to right and not right to left. It is only natural for anyone doing this for the first time to write and record the values from left to right. You can start writing and recording the numbers from right to left and your beginning value would result in 14644, read the meter again in two weeks 14645, and two weeks later 14646. This time when you perform your calculations you are subtracting 14646 minus 14644 for a total of 2 kWh in usage for the month. Dream on!

The simplest way to record and track your electrical meter reading is to do what you have been taught to do and is natural for most people. Simply, read, write and record the values from left to right. You would have naturally written a starting or most recent value of 14646 and subtract the oldest recorded reading of 14644, in this case from our hypothetical values in Figure 5 resulting in the same 2 kWh in usage for the month. Your utility bill should indicate whether that last meter reading by your utility company is an actual or estimated meter reading. In any case, you now have the information you need to track your electrical usage and estimate your monthly utility bill with a minimum error rate, excluding local tax, state tax, surcharges and miscellaneous fees. You will also be able to get an idea of what is normal usage for your household.

Davids Meter Readings with Incorrect and Correct Values

Date	Reading	Time	kWh Usage
Incorrect Recording of Meter Reading Result			
2/11/2010	14146	319pm	
2/15/2010	86351	626am	Unable to determine
2/15/2010	98452	305pm	Unable to determine
2/16/2010	14406	1118am	84046 ?
2/16/2010	71452	314pm	Unable to determine
Correct Recording of Meter Readings Result			
3/19/2010	14563	808am	---
3/20/2010	14567	856am	4
3/21/2010	14571	1054am	4
3/22/2010	14575	950am	4
3/23/2010	14577	746am	2

Source: Davids Meter Tracking Record Excerpts

David's Stone

Electric utilities power the appliances and comforts in our homes such as heating, air conditioning, refrigerators, stoves, dishwashers, washers, dryers, water heater, televisions, stereos, computers, and lighting. We are a nation of consumption and corporations are making billions because of it. Preparing to take a stand and fight back is a task requiring risk, discipline, peer pressure, commentary, frugality, trial and error, imagination, common sense, and jury rigging. If, you are willing to employ some, all, or a combination of these techniques you take the responsibility. It is likely some of these suggestions are provided by your own utility company, have been reported in your local news paper, your local nightly news cast, or you have seen it via an Internet search.

Seasonally, heating or air conditioning demand can vary according to geographic location and you or your familys preferences and tolerances. Generally, it is easier to stay warm than it is to stay cool. The recommended thermostat setting in summer should not be below 78 degrees Fahrenheit and in winter not above 68 degrees (About.com, 2010). Interested in saving more on your utility bill without recurring costs? You can increase the amount of clothing you are wearing, invest in thermal underwear, invest in sleeping bags, invest in a down feather bed comforter, sleep with your family, sleep with your pet(s), turn off the heat when you are not at home and when you go to sleep during the winter months. This requires common sense, if it is unbearable and you risk freezing to death do not be stupid and turn your heat off. Conversely, during the summer wear light clothing and set your thermostat at a temperature where you can detect a noticeable difference. For example, if it is 100 degrees Fahrenheit and high humidity, your body will likely detect a noticeable difference around 90 degrees Fahrenheit. Obviously if the setting is causing you severe physical distress that you or your family are not able to tolerate experiment with the thermostat and temperature settings until you can establish a sustainable threshold. Additionally, turn off the air conditioning unit if you are not at home.

Laundry is a never ending task and there is a sock monster. This is a simple saver with potential benefits. You can wash your clothes using cold water eliminating the use on the electric hot water heater. The winter months, this is debatable and depends on where your dryer is located in your home. The dryer might be in a location in your home where it acts as an agent for heating your home. Why do you have the heat on at the same time? Clothes do not have to be dried in a dryer during the winter months you can hang them over your bathtub or run a clothes line in your basement. The spring, summer, and fall season hang them outside. It worked for many people before dryers came along.

Is your stove gas or electric? If, you have a gas stove you can eliminate using your dishwasher and the hot water heater. You can boil enough water to wash your dishes by hand. Do not boil the water to the point where you burn your hands in the sink. If you have any concerns about using hot water invest in a pair of those dishwashing gloves to protect your hands and use pot holders to transport the pots of hot water. You can have one sink for washing and one for rinsing. You may have to replenish both sinks depending on how many dishes you have. Once again, remember boiling this water is putting heat in your home from the stove flame and as hot water vapor. Granted doing dishes is a chore but if you are not turning your heat on this provides an excellent opportunity to get yourself warmed up and get a task completed when it is cold.

Televisions, computers, stereos and lighting are fixtures in our homes. If, you are watching television why do you have your lights on in other parts of your home? If, you are using your computer why do you have lights on in other parts of your home? The television and computer screen emit sufficient light to navigate yourself within your home and you should be aware of how your furniture is arranged. Invest in a battery operated camping lantern, a propane camping lantern, a flashlight or candles. You can turn off the lights. If, you are not using a particular appliance pull the plug or invest in a multi plug surge protector with the little on off switch. You can invest in a wind up alarm clock or use the alarm on your cell phone. Charge the cell phone on your drive to work using a car charger.

Your hot water heater may be electric or gas. If you have an electric hot water heater you can purchase a timer and set it to turn on and off at preset times this stops it from running 24/7. You can also just turn it off and create designated hot shower days and take sponge baths by boiling water. Additionally, you can limit hot showers to 7-9 minutes.

Refrigeration of food and beverages is arguably the most important appliance in a home. The Federal Government has published guidelines for the public regarding refrigeration and safe food handling. They suggest For safety, it is important to verify the temperature of the refrigerator. Refrigerators should be set to maintain a temperature of 40 degrees F or below. An appliance thermometer can be kept in the refrigerator to monitor the temperature. This can be critical in the event of a power outage. When the power goes back on, if the refrigerator is still 40 degrees F, the food is safe. Foods held at temperatures above 40 degrees F for more than two hours should not be consumed. Appliance thermometers are specifically designed to provide accuracy at cold temperatures. Be sure refrigerator/freezer doors are closed tightly at all times. Don not open refrigerator/freezer doors more often than necessary and close them as soon as possible (US Department of Agriculture, 2010). This is perhaps the most extreme and riskiest action to pursue in reducing electrical usage. Should you elect to use this as an option toward reducing your electric consumption you do this from an informed state and solely responsible for any possible negative health effects. It might be beneficial to keep several gallons of frozen water in your freezer depending on the available room. Turn off the refrigerator.

You can take additional steps using various alternative actions. The winter months are cold and allowing the sun to shine into your house will help slightly. You will have to draw the shades or curtains about an hour prior to sundown to prevent a loss of heat. The summer months you want to reverse yourself and keep the shades and curtain drawn, opening windows to allow any possible breeze to circulate. Everyone loves to BBQ. If you have experienced a Hurricane and the aftermath BBQ becomes old and boring for a prolonged period of time. If you have an electric stove then BBQ can be a wonderful treat and saving.

Energy auditing is a procedure that some utility companies will offer their customers as a free service. It is supposed to help you identify areas in your home that are potential causes of energy inefficiency. This can include insulation, duct work, weather stripping, window types, and age of heavy appliances. Davids audit revealed he should get some duct work performed. He has to pay the electric bill first.

This is an effective method to cutting your electrical usage. Here is the proof. ***These actions resulted in a 56.5% reduction in electrical usage from the previous month and an 83.65% reduction in electrical usage from the previous year.***

Historical Data	Last Month	1 Yr Ago	KWH This Month	KWH Per Day
2/04-3/02/10	7393	1679	875	34
3/02-4/01/10	875	253	143	5
4/02-5/03/10	143	----	----	----

Source: Davids Electric Bill

Your monthly electrical expense in dollars will coincide with this reduction in electrical usage. Seriously, do you really need all those electrical gadgets and appliances using electricity while you are at work, the kids are in school, or when you are sleeping? NO, NO, and NO. Do you need all your electrical users running when you go shopping or out to dinner? NO. The power goes off at 8pm and comes on again at 8am and shut it off at the breaker box. Shut it off whenever you leave your home.

       This is not an unusual scenario for many people to find themselves in todays economy. You do have a voice so speak up loudly. You do have control of what is under your own domain. You can help yourself and possibly others. Write letters, Email and make phone calls to your State Representatives, your Congressional Representatives, CEOs of your Utility Company, your Public Service Commission, and your local news media. You are not alone in your thoughts and there are people in your community who are compassionate, who understand, who are in a position to help, who do have the power to effect and create change for the welfare of all people. You have to let them know. Perhaps, it is time for an official complaint in writing to the PSC. Perhaps, it is time for an official complaint in writing to State Legislators.

Conclusions

There are shortcomings in this presentation. First, this is an extreme method in reducing your electrical usage and it may not benefit some people at all. For example, you might live in a multi-housing complex and the electric may be included in your monthly rent, you may use natural gas or propane. You may spend less than 1.0% of your monthly income on your electric utility bill. This approach is seasonal and heat and humidity are not as easy to adjust for or control. You may just find this approach to be too extreme and unrealistic for your lifestyle. Second, a lot of emphasis was placed on corporate revenue in the billions and corporate expenses were not taken into account regarding the bookkeeping concepts of assets and liabilities, allowed deductions, and the Federal and State estimated taxes they are required to pay on a quarterly basis. Corporate America can afford it when it benefits them but they will tell you it cannot be done when it benefits the consumer. Why not? Finally, while looking at these billions of revenue circulating from one hand to another and then back again it struck me, without words to describe or explain other than; economically we are living in a state of revolving credit and a haunting repeat of Enron sits just over the horizon. Goliath may be keeping the revolving door in motion by pure force of energy but there are too many Davids being created and that revolving door is going to jam and come to a screeching halt.

Appendix Resources PSC and VOC

Public Service Commission

National Resource	National Association of Regulatory Utility Commissioners URL
USA Public Service Commissions	http://www.naruc.org/commissions.cfm

Source: (National Association of Regulatory Utility Commissioners, 2010)

Victim of Crime

National Resource	Crime Victims Assistance Resources URL
USA Victims of Crime	http://www.crimevictims.gov/crime.html

Source: (Office for Victims of Crime, 2010)

Appendix Utilities

American Electrical Power and State Unemployment Rate

Symbol	Subsidiary Name	State	Unemployment Rate
AEP	AEP Ohio	OH	10.9%
	AEP Texas	TX	8.2%
	Indiana Michigan Power	IN	10.0%
		MI	14.1%
	Kentucky Power	TN	10.7%
	Appalachian Power	WV	9.5%
Revenue 2009			13.5 Billion

Source of Unemployment Statistics: (Bureau of Labor Statistics, 2010)

Dominion Resources and State Unemployment Rate

Symbol	Subsidiary	State	Unemployment Rate
D	Dominion North Carolina Power	NC	11.2%
	Dominion Virginia Power	VA	7.2%
Revenue 2009			15.1 Billion

Source of Unemployment Statistics: (Bureau of Labor Statistics, 2010)

Duke Energy Corporation and State Unemployment Rate

Symbol	Subsidiary	State	Unemployment Rate
DUK	Duke Energy of Indiana	IN	10.0%
	Duke Energy Carolinas	NC	11.2%
		SC	12.5%
	Duke Energy Ohio	OH	10.9%
	Duke Energy Kentucky	KY	10.9%
Revenue 2009			12.7 Billion

Source of Unemployment Statistics: (Bureau of Labor Statistics, 2010)

Entergy Corporation and State Unemployment Rate

Symbol	Subsidiary	State	Unemployment Rate
ETR	Entergy Arkansas	ARK	7.7%
	Entergy Gulf States Louisiana		
	Entergy Mississippi	MS	14.1%
	Entergy Louisiana	LA	7.3%
	Entergy New Orleans		
	Entergy Texas	TX	8.2%
Revenue 2009			6.7 Billion

Source of Unemployment Statistics: (Bureau of Labor Statistics, 2010)

Edison International and State Unemployment Rate

Symbol	Subsidiary	State	Unemployment Rate
EIX	Edison International	CA	12.5%
Revenue 2009			12.4 Billion

Source of Unemployment Statistics: (Bureau of Labor Statistics, 2010)

FPL Group and State Unemployment Rate

Symbol	Subsidiary	State	Unemployment Rate
FPL	Florida Power and Light	FL	12.2%
Revenue 2009			15.6 Billion

Source of Unemployment Statistics: (Bureau of Labor Statistics, 2010)

First Energy Corporation and State Unemployment Rate

Symbol	Subsidiary	State	Unemployment Rate
FE	Jersey Central Power and Light	NJ	10.0%
	Metropolitan Edison Company	PA	8.8%
	Ohio Edison Company	OH	10.9%
	Pennsylvania Electric Company	PA	8.8%
	Pennsylvania Power Company	PA	8.8%
	The Cleveland Electric Illuminating Company	OH	10.9%
Revenue 2009			13 Billion

Source of Unemployment Statistics: (Bureau of Labor Statistics, 2010)

Southern Company and State Unemployment Rate

Symbol	Subsidiary	State	Unemployment Rate
SO	Alabama Power	AL	11.1%
	Georgia Power	GA	10.5%
	Gulf Power	FL	12.2%
	Mississippi Power	MS	14.1%
	Southern Company Generation		
	Southern Nuclear		
	Southern LINC/Telecom		
Revenue 2009			15.7 Billion

Source of Unemployment Statistics: (Bureau of Labor Statistics, 2010)

Abbreviations

AEP- American Electric Power, Inc.
BP- British Petroleum
COP- Conoco Phillips Corporation
COLA- Cost of Living Allowance
CSU- Crime Scene Unit
CVX- Chevron Corporation
D- Dominion Resources Inc.
DIY- Do It Yourself
DUK- Duke Energy Corporation
EIX- Edison International Corporation
FE- First Energy Corporation
FPSC- Florida Public Service Commission
FPL- FPL Group, Inc.
ETR- Entergy Corporation
IRA- Individual Retirement Account
kWh- kilowatt hours
PSC- Public Service Commission
SO- Southern Company
STT- State Street Corporation
VOC- Victim of Crime
VLO- Valero Energy Corporation
XOM- Exxon Mobil Corporation

List of Figures

Notes

Bibliography

About.com. (2010, March 20). *Setting your thermostat for maximum Energy Savings*. Retrieved March 20, 2010, from About.com: Saving Energy: http://saveenergy.about.com/od/homecooling/qt/termostatsettin.htm

American Electric Power. (2010, March 19). *American Electric Power Home Page*. Retrieved March 19, 2010, from American Electric Power Home Page: http://www.aep.com/

Angier, D. (2008, June 20). *Gulf Power Seeks Rate Hike*. Retrieved March 23, 2010, from Panama City New Herald : http://www.newsherald.com/news/company-4556-power-fuel.html

Article Cube. (2010, March 21). *Types of Electric Meters-Steve Hallows*. Retrieved March 21, 2010, from Article Cube Website: http://www.articlecube.com/Article/Types-of-Electric-Meters/630197

Associated Press. (2005, November 9). *In Heated Hearings, oil bosses defend big profits*. Retrieved March 28, 2010, from Oil & Energy- MSNBC.com: http://www.msnbc.msn.com/id/9970294/

Associated Press. (2010, March 15). *State Street spent $270,000 lobbying gov't in 4Q*. Retrieved March 18, 2010, from Yahoo Finance: http://finance.yahoo.com/news/State-Street-spent-270000-apf-2932802458.html?x=0&.v=1

Bureau of Labor Statistics. (2010, March 29). *List of U.S. states by Unemployment Rate*. Retrieved March 29, 2010, from Wikipedia-The Free Encyclopedia: http://en.wikipedia.org/wiki/List_of_U.S._states_by_unemployment_rate

Bureau of Labor Statistics. (2010, March 19). *List of U.S. states by unemployment rate-Wikipedia the free encyclopedia*. Retrieved March 19, 2010, from Wikipedia-The free encyclopedia: http://en.wikipedia.org/wiki/List_of_U.S._states_by_unemployment_rate

Clean Energy.Org. (2009, October 19). *Will the FLorida Public Service Commission Stick with the Status Quo on Efficiency?* Retrieved April 7, 2010, from Clean Energy Foorprints-Archive: http://blog.cleanenergy.org/2009/10/15/will-the-florida-public-service-commission-stick-with-the-status-quo-on-efficiency/

Dominion Companies. (2010, March 19). *Dominion Companies-About Us*. Retrieved March 19, 2010, from Dominion Resources Web Site: http://www.dom.com/about/companies/index.jsp

Duke Energy Corporation. (2010, March 19). *Duke Energy-About Us-Leadership*. Retrieved March 19, 2010, from Duke Energy Corporate Website: http://www.duke-energy.com/about-us/leaders.asp

E*Trade. (2010, March 18). Retrieved March 18, 2010, from E*Trade Financial Web site: http://www.etrade.com

Edison International. (2010, March 19). *Edison International-Our Company-Edison International Leadership*. Retrieved March 19, 2010, from Edison International Corporate Web site: http://www.edison.com/ourcompany/management.asp

Entergy Corporation. (2010, March 19). *Entergy-About Entergy*. Retrieved March 19, 20, from Entergy Corporation Web Site: http://www.entergy.com/about_entergy/company_links.aspx

First Energy Corporate. (2010, March 19). *First Energy Electric Operating Companies*. Retrieved March 19, 2010, from First Energy Corporate Web site: http://www.firstenergycorp.com/corporate/Operating_Companies/index.html

Florida Attorney General. (2010, March 29). *Crime Victim's Services*. Retrieved March 29, 2010, from Office of the Attorney General of Florida: http://myfloridalegal.com/pages.nsf/Main/B371D29EBE5C9774852 5749C00518B58

Florida Attorney General. (2010, March 29). *Crime Victims' Services*. Retrieved March 29, 2010, from Office of the Attorney General of Florida: http://myfloridalegal.com/pages.nsf/main/a13e1518920d0de685256cc6004bd490!OpenDocument

Florida Attorney General. (2010, March 29). *Crime Victims's Service-Resources*. Retrieved March 29, 2010, from Office of the Attorney General of Florida: http://myfloridalegal.com/pages.nsf/Main/2BDCBF1BD04DDBFF8525749C004F4B42

Florida Attorney General. (2010, March 29). *Victim Services Directory*. Retrieved March 29, 2010, from Office of the Attorney General of Florida: http://myfloridalegal.com/directory

Florida Department of State. (2010, March 25). *Florida Administrative Weekly & Florida Administrative Code*. Retrieved March 25, 2010, from Div. 25: Departmental-Florida Administrative Rules, Law, Code, Register-FAC,FAW, eRulemaki: https://www.flrules.org/gateway/Division.asp?DivID=396

Florida Department of State. (2010, March 25). *Florida Administrative Weekly & Florida Administrative Weekly*. Retrieved March 25, 2010, from 25-6: Electric Service by Electric Public Utilities-Florida Administrative Rules, Laws, Code: https://www.flrules.org/gateway/ChapterHome.asp?Chapter=25-6

Florida Department of State. (2010, March 25 25). *Florida Adminsitrative Weekly & Adminsitrative Code*. Retrieved March 25, 2010, from 25-6: Electric Service by Electric Public Utilities- Florida Administrative Rules, Law, Code: https://www.flrules.org/gateway/ChapterHome.asp?Chapter=25-6

FPL Group. (2010, March 29). *FPL Group: About Us*. Retrieved March 29, 2010, from FPL Group Corporate Web Site: http://www.fplgroup.com/about/contents/about_us.shtml

Gulf Power. (2009, April 30). *FERC Financial Report*. Retrieved March 21, 2010, from My Florida Public Service Commission: http://www.psc.state.fl.us/library/financials/EI804-DOCS/ANNUAL-REPORTS/EI804-08-AR.PDF

Hewlett Packard. (2001, September 3). *HP Press Release: HEWLETT-PACKARD and COMPAQ Agree To Merge, Creating $87 Billion Global Technology Leader* . Retrieved March 20, 2010, from Hewlett Packard Corporation Web site: http://www.hp.com/hpinfo/newsroom/press/2001/010904a.html

Market Watch-The Wall Street Journal. (2010, January 14). *Updates, advisories and Surprises*. Retrieved April 7, 2010, from FPL trims $10 billion in projects after rate case : http://www.marketwatch.com/story/updates-advisories-and-surprises-2010-01-14

Merriam-Webster. (2010, March 20). *Bribe-Definiion and More from the Merriam-Webster Free Dictionary*. Retrieved March 20, 2010, from Merriam-Webster: http://www.merriam-webster.com/dictionary/bribe

Merriam-Webster. (2010, March 20). *Capitalism-Definition and More from the Free Merriam-Webster Dictionary*. Retrieved March 20, 2010, from Merriam-Webster: http://www.merriam-webster.com/dictionary/capitalism

Merriam-Webster. (2010, March 20). *Competition-Definitions and More from the Free Merriam-Webster Dictionary*. Retrieved March 20, 2010, from Merriam-Webster: http://www.merriam-webster.com/dictionary/competition

Merriam-Webster. (2010, March 20). *Crime against humanity-Definition and More from the Free Merriam-Webster Dictionary*. Retrieved March 20, 2010, from Merriam-Webster: http://www.merriam-webster.com/dictionary/crime%20against%20humanity

Merriam-Webster. (2010, March 20). *Extortion-Definition and More from the Free Merriam-Webster Dictionary*. Retrieved March 20, 2010, from Merriam-Webster: http://www.merriam-webster.com/dictionary/extortion

Merriam-Webster. (2010, March 20). *Free market-Definition and More from the Free Merriam-Webster Dictionary*. Retrieved March 20, 2010, from Merriam-Webster: http://www.merriam-webster.com/dictionary/free%20market

Merriam-Webster. (2010, March 20). *Lobyist-Definition and More from the Free Merriam-Webster Dictionary*. Retrieved March 20, 2010, from Merriam Webster: http://www.merriam-webster.com/dictionary/lobbyist

Merriam-Webster. (2010, March 20). *Meriam-Webster*. Retrieved March 20, 2010, from Monopoly-Definition and More from the Free Merriam Webster Dictionary: http://www.merriam-webster.com/dictionary/monopoly

My Florida Public Service Commission. (2010, March 21). *Consumer Assisstance-Public Service Commission*. Retrieved March 21, 2010, from My Florida Public Service Commission: http://www.psc.state.fl.us/consumers/

My Florida Public Service Commission. (2010, March 21). *Div. 25 Departmental-Florida Administrative Rules, Law, Code,Register-FAC, FAW, eRulemaki*. Retrieved March 21, 2010, from Public Service Commission Web Site: https://www.flrules.org/gateway/Division.asp?DivID=396

My Florida Public Service Commission. (2010, March 21).
Welcome to the PSC Web Site. Retrieved March 21, 2010, from
Public Service Commission Commision: http://www.psc.state.fl.us/

My Florida Public Service Commission. (2010, March 21).
When To Call the Florida Public Service Commission. Retrieved
March 21, 2010, from My Florida Public Service Commission:
http://www.psc.state.fl.us/publications/consumer/brochure/When_to
_Call_the_PSC.pdf

National Association of Regulatory Utility Commissioners.
(2010, March 29). *National Association of Regulatory Utility
Commissioners*. Retrieved March 29, 2010, from National
Association of Regulatory Utility Commissioners:
http://www.naruc.org/commissions.cfm

Office for Victims of Crime. (2010, March 29). *Crime Victims*.
Retrieved March 29, 2010, from Office for Vistims of Crime:
http://www.crimevictims.gov/crime.html

Seco Energy. (2010, March 5). *How to read your electric meter*.
Retrieved March 21, 2010, from Seco Energy Corporation:
http://www.secoenergy.com/readmeter.html

Silver, J. A. (2010, March 28). *Movie Day at the Supreme Court
or "I know it when I see it": A history of the Definition of Obscenity*.
Retrieved March 28, 2010, from Find Law for Legal Professionals:
http://library.findlaw.com/2003/May/15/132747.html

State Street Corporate. (2009, June 17). *Press Release-State
Street Repays $2 Billion in Tarp Funds*. Retrieved March 19, 2010,
from State Street Corporation Web site:
http://pr.statestreet.com/us/en/20090617_1.html

The Southern Company. (2010, March 19). *Company
Executives-Southern Company*. Retrieved March 19, 2010, from
Southern Company Website:
http://www.southerncompany.com/aboutus/execs.aspx

US Department of Agriculture. (2010, March 20). *Refrigeration & Food Safey*. Retrieved March 20, 2010, from US Department of Agriculture: http://www.fsis.usda.gov/fact_sheets/Refrigeration_&_Food_Safety/index.asp

Wikipedia. (2010, March 20). *Dividing territories-Wikipedia the free encyclopedia*. Retrieved March 20, 2010, from Wikipedia: http://en.wikipedia.org/wiki/Dividing_territories

Wikipedia. (2001, October). *Enron scandal-Wikipedia, the free encylopedia*. Retrieved April 2, 2010, from Wikipedia, The Free Encylcopedia: http://en.wikipedia.org/wiki/Enron_scandal

Wikipedia. (2010, March 20). *Monopoly-the free encyclopedia*. Retrieved March 20, 2010, from Wikipedia: http://en.wikipedia.org/wiki/Monopoly

Wikipedia. (2010, March 22). *Pensions-Wikipedia, the free encyclopedia*. Retrieved March 22, 2010, from Wikpedia-the free encyclopedia: http://en.wikipedia.org/wiki/Pension

Wikipedia. (2010, March 22). *Social Security Administration-Wikipedia the free encyclopedia*. Retrieved March 22, 2010, from Wikipedia-the free encyclopedia: http://en.wikipedia.org/wiki/Social_Security_Administration

Wikipedia. (2010, March 22). *The Jungle-Wikipedia the free Encyclopedia*. Retrieved March 22, 2010, from Wikipedia-the free Encyclopedia: http://en.wikipedia.org/wiki/The_Jungle

Wikipedia. (2010, March 22). *United States Department of Labor-Wikipedia the free Encyclopedia*. Retrieved March 22, 2010, from Wikipedia-the Free Encyclopedia: http://en.wikipedia.org/wiki/US_Department_of_Labor

Yahoo . (2010, March 20). *Yahoo Finance*. Retrieved March 20, 2010, from Yahoo Finance Web site Investing: http://finance.yahoo.com/q?s=BP

Yahoo Finance. (2010, March 18). *Industry Center-Electric Utilities-Leaders and Laggards*. Retrieved March 18, 2010, from Industry Center-Electric Utilities: http://biz.yahoo.com/ic/ll/911mkt.html

Yahoo Finance. (2010, March 18). *STT:Major Holders for State Street Corporation Common-Yahoo Finance*. Retrieved March 19, 2010, from Yahoo Finance: http://finance.yahoo.com/q/mh?s=STT

Zacks Equity Research. (2010, March 4). *State Street Pays Leaving CEO $5.4M*. Retrieved March 18, 2010, from Yahoo Finance: http://finance.yahoo.com/news/State-Street-Pays-Leaving-CEO-zacks-1352425227.html?x=0&.v=1

www.ingramcontent.com/pod-product-compliance
Lightning Source LLC
Chambersburg PA
CBHW071247170526
45165CB00003B/1274